Feathers
&
Rainbows

Acknowledgements

My husband Trevor and I would like to dedicate this book to our families, our friends and the medical teams who supported us on our journey. In particular, I'd like to thank my grown-up children Ellie and Joel, for understanding and reminding me how strong I can be. They supported me through the hardest times of my life. I'd also like to thank all of the maternity, labour, gynaecology, and IVF experts as well as the holistic therapists who helped with our fertility journey. An additional, huge thank you to everyone who donated to our baby Bobby's *Just Giving* page which raised funds for St Richard's hospital in Chichester to support parents of babies born sleeping. These funds not only helped the hospital but gave us something positive to focus on in the lead-up to Bobby's funeral. We appreciated it beyond words.

We also have a network of people who surround us – you really know who your besties are in times of trouble. I have individually detailed how these people helped us get through the hardest time of our lives at the end of our story. I hope that this book will offer guidance and comfort to those experiencing fertility issues, the trauma of miscarriages and babies born sleeping. It is one of the worst things that anybody will ever have to go through so if this has happened to you, remember, **you are not alone.**

#feathersandrainbows #babyloss #miscarriage #stillbirth #IVF

Contents:

PART FIVE

PART SIX

APPENDIX:

How can we ever thank those who helped us on our journey?

FOREWORD

Why Feathers and why Rainbows?

Why Feathers?

I believe that baby Bobby, our angel, our baby born sleeping, drops or leaves us white feathers.

TV presenter Gloria Hunniford lost her daughter Caron to cancer when she was 41. I remember reading an article by Gloria about a single white feather being an angel's calling card.

From that moment, so many white feathers have appeared, and I really believe they're Bobby saying 'Hi' and giving me a sign he's alright. Gloria spoke about this in Daily Mail online:

"Nine months after Caron died from breast cancer in 2004, my husband Stephen and I took her sons Gabriel and Charlie to Disneyland. We were walking along the wet platform to the train and my mood was as miserable as the weather. Caron should have been there with us. All of a sudden, a beautiful white feather landed at my feet. Caron had been fascinated with angels ever since she made a documentary about them and would insist, 'There are angels for everything, and you just have to ask.' She believed implicitly that if you find a single feather it is an angel's calling card – a sign that they're there with you."

Gloria Hunniford, DailyMail.co.uk 25th January 2020

This stayed with me, buried deep in my sub-consciousness. I was reminded one day when a white feather fell on my face as I was walking our two dogs, Bella the Beagle and Bonita the Border Collie.

I had been chatting to baby Bobby in my head as we stomped around the muddy field near our house, asking how he was, telling him about my day, and begging him to come back. At that time, I'd convinced myself that we would have another baby (a rainbow baby), Bobby would be back and his soul would be within his or her body.

And there it was – a single white feather - a sign that someone, or better still Bobby, had heard me. I still have that feather as a reminder never to give up hope.

Why Rainbows? I have always loved and had a fascination for rainbows. I've had a few near misses while driving because I've spotted a rainbow and struggled to draw my eyes away. They are so beautiful and mysterious.

After we lost our baby Bobby, one of Trevor's friends confided a similar experience before he'd had another baby - his rainbow baby. This term is used for babies born to parents following a baby loss. The rainbow became more than fascination for us; it was a symbol of hope and suddenly we both saw rainbows everywhere, in the sky, on items in shops, on Facebook posts.

When Covid-19 hit, the rainbow symbolised hope for the whole world and again they were everywhere, in shop windows, on company logos, TV and websites. It was incredible and made me even more certain that we would indeed have our Rainbow Baby.

INTRODUCTION

Why I wanted more children

I mention my age throughout this story because age is relevant to fertility issues. I was 38 when Trevor and I started trying for a baby and five years on, we were still on our fertility journey.

Time flies by when you are trying for a baby or having IVF and there is a lot of waiting involved. If you are near or into your 40s there can be a sense of panic about your body's ability to conceive. Unfortunately, there is nothing anyone can do when it comes to nature's timing.

I'm a normal girl, well woman, divorced with two children, Ellie and Joel.

When I was 35 in the autumn of 2012, Ellie was 13, Joel was 11, and I had just separated from their father. I was shopping with Mum one day and she asked, 'Why don't you have more children?'

'Are you crazy Mum? Not a chance! I couldn't put my body through that again!'

But for some reason, that moment never left me. My mum loved the idea of more grandchildren and as an only child there was only me to provide them. I couldn't blame her for trying.

I had been through a dreadful marital separation. My ex-husband and I had reluctantly agreed to have the children 50% of the time each. This situation could easily be the topic for another book but out of love and respect for my children that won't happen.

Over time, the trauma of our family separation and the pain of my children spending half their lives with their father subsided.
I missed them terribly when they were gone but also realised that as Ellie and Joel were growing up so quickly, I missed having little children around.
Children are so much fun; they keep your mind young.
I began entertaining the idea of having more but was worried I wouldn't be physically strong enough. In addition, I would need to be in a stable relationship before even considering it. But at the time I felt the need to release some steam and have fun before settling down again. I had a few more frogs to kiss before I found my prince.

'Bring on the fun times!' became my Skype, WhatsApp, and Facebook statuses. And fun times I had! I reconnected with friends when the children were at their dad's and filled my diary with fun events. I joined dating sites, which weren't successful to start with but got me out meeting new people.

I didn't enjoy living alone so I quickly found a lodger who became a perfect companion and party partner which helped ease the feeling of loneliness. We had a lot of fun together.

We became friendly with local bars and lived life to the full. It was a rare occasion for us to stay in during the evenings but when we did it would be with friends and a few bottles of wine. I worked hard as a full-time marketer but played hard too. It was just what I needed to 'find myself' again.

I did have a couple of unsuccessful relationships with men who had children. The first had five and seven-year-old boys while the second had a daughter aged around eight. I enjoyed spending time with them and in fact I missed the children more than their fathers after the relationships ended.

I began to wonder whether having more children myself was a silly idea and perhaps it would be more practical to adopt. I already had my own son and daughter, why not help children already in the world? I could do this on my own – no man required (even easier, I thought!) I started to research adoption and became convinced this was my new calling.

PART ONE

Chapter One: Meeting my Prince

At thirty-eight I met the man of my dreams through a dating app. Trevor was forty-nine, well forty-eight until our second date which fell on his birthday. On our first date, as I walked away from my car towards the pub where we were meeting, I spotted the most beautiful dog and knew she was Trevor's Border Collie Bonita. It was love at first sight.

Then came her "dad", Trevor.

'This could work', I thought. He had brown hair, was slightly taller than me, and had a mysterious, handsome look. We got on well instantly. I was completely enthralled with Trevor for the whole three hours of our date.

We had such a fabulous night, talking about everything and anything: our jobs, families and friends, hobbies. We laughed so much that time flew by and before I knew it, it was time to say goodbye.

Trevor walked me to my car and opened the door for me, which I loved as it made me feel like a lady. This was something he continued to do for months until I told him it was very sweet but not needed.

That night was the beginning of our incredible journey together.

It only took a few more dates before we knew this was it. On our third date, Trevor booked us a table at a Spanish restaurant and we had tapas with two bottles of wine (admittedly it might have been three!).

That night, we spoke about children. Trevor explained that he'd always wanted them and his ex-wife had originally told him that she had wanted them but in reality, she didn't, which was a reason they had separated. He felt he had missed his chance. It was then that I realised that maybe having more children with this gorgeous man was meant to be.

It took me time to introduce Trevor to my family. My daughter Ellie was the first to meet him; I introduced him as being my friend at a Mini Cooper race at Brooklands racecourse, an event that was being recorded for the Guinness Book of World Records.

Trevor had been hired to photograph the event and managed to get Ellie and I access to watch. He took an amazing picture of myself and Ellie. Later that day she said, "He's nice mum, a good one I'd say!"

We gradually met each other's friends and family while we focused on having fun, as though we were making up for not spending the last 20 years together. Everything felt perfect.

Chapter Two: Our Fertility Journey Begins

We were so excited having made the decision to have a family of our own and wanted to get started, but our fertility journey was complicated from the beginning.

The first step was to have my coil removed. Simple, right? Unfortunately not.

It took four months and four doctors' as well as an appointment at the local hospital where the doctor explained that the strings had slipped up into my cervical canal and we'd need an ultrasound appointment to remove the coil with forceps.

By this time, I was already starting to feel the urgency as the days, weeks and months flew past and still I was not pregnant as my 40th birthday loomed.

Our fifth and final appointment took another four weeks and I found myself, legs straddled over stirrups, in what I now call the *glamour chair*. I had no idea there were to be many appointments like this ahead of us.

Then finally, the doctor announced, 'its out!'

At last, we could start trying for our baby.

We thought that was our only hurdle but little did we know that it was just one tiny hill in front of the huge mountains ahead of us.

Chapter Three: Our Lives Merging

We travelled a lot the following year and Trevor's photography job took us as far as Bali to photograph a celebrity. The local people in Bali were lovely and couldn't do enough for us. We took many trips.... our favourite was a boat trip with dinner and dancing.

We stopped in Singapore for one night only on the way home – I don't think we slept as we preferred to go and tick off our list of sights to see!

We visited Marina Bay Sands, went on a river boat, visited Raffles, had a Singapore Sling cocktail, ate monkey nuts and crushed the shells on the floor, apparently that's the thing to do there!

On our return, I changed jobs a few times trying to find something I enjoyed and which paid the right salary while I was still buying and renovating properties.

My friends were all approaching their 40th birthdays (as was I) while Trevor's friends were approaching their 50s, plus there were weddings and parties aplenty. I also spent time with Ellie and Joel; precious memories which I will always treasure.

PART TWO

Chapter Four: Our First Pregnancy

Not long after I turned 40, while we were having such good times, I constantly hoped to fall pregnant. I loved that we were enjoying each other and all these experiences together before our baby came along.

Then, one day I felt strange and realised that my period was late. I ran to the bathroom and took a pregnancy test.

There it was – the second line! I couldn't believe it and was bursting to tell Trevor.

I called him, shaking with excitement and suggested we go to the Queens Head, where we had our first date. As soon as we sat down at the table, I couldn't wait any more. I blurted out: 'I'm pregnant babe!' I was so excited I had butterflies in my stomach. 'Are you sure?' he said, with wide eyes. 'Yes! I did a test today. I've got another one in my bag, just to be sure. Shall I take it?"

His face lit up and I went to the ladies to take the test. I put it straight in my bag without looking so we could view the result together.

Trevor's eyes almost burned holes in mine as we waited for the result. When we finally looked, there it was – the second line! We spent the rest of the evening smiling from ear to ear.

We didn't want to tell anybody until the eight-week point, past the miscarriage danger zone. Ellie and Joel were at the age when bad news would hurt and they had experienced so much disappointment with their family break-up. Ellie was studying for her A-levels and Joel was not having an easy, time so I wanted to deliver the news carefully.

There was a lot of change already happening for them; Trevor and I planned to move in together and had found a house to rent nearby with lovely rooms for them both.

I did tell my best friend, Tiff. She wasn't expecting to hear such news and her excited shrieking almost made the phone explode!

I decided to wait and tell Mum during our short city break in Rome, which had been her birthday present.

By then, I was just over eight weeks pregnant. I asked the doctor if it was safe to fly and she said it was. I was still exercising and doing all the things advised by medics, but as I was 40, and that meant high-risk, I would need to be watched closely through my pregnancy.

Mum loved Rome. It was her first time in Italy and being Irish Catholic she had dreamed of seeing the Pope and Vatican City. We went to The Ivy restaurant on our first evening, where I planned to tell her our good news.

The restaurant was beautiful and when the waiter came to take our drinks order, Mum ordered a glass of wine and I asked for an orange juice.

"Are you sure you wouldn't like a glass of wine?" she asked when the waiter left to organise the drinks. I couldn't wait another minute to tell her.

"I'm pregnant," I said.

I had to say it a couple of times before it sank in. She was over the moon, smiling from ear to ear. "That's amazing, congratulations!" She was so excited about the prospect of being a nana again.

I kept up my fitness routine of going for a morning jog but on the last morning of the holiday, when I headed for the shower, I saw blood in my underwear.

Horror struck and I could feel my heart beat faster as tears welled.

I couldn't tell mum and we were away from home, and away from Trevor. What would I tell him? I called him and I could hear the worry in his voice. I called the emergency number for my midwife, who said, 'Try not to worry. Go to A&E on your way home so we can take a look.' It didn't occur to me to go to the hospital in Italy as I was just hours away from Heathrow.

I acted normally and carried on as if nothing was happening because I didn't want to break mum's heart, but at that moment mine was shattering.

The taxi ride to the airport was bumpy and mum kept tutting that the shaking was no good for me and that the driver should take more care.

Trevor collected us from the airport and after dropping mum home, we headed to the hospital. The dread left me unable to speak.

At A&E we had to wait in a cubicle. A doctor examined me but she was unable to tell us anything other than to advise me to take things easy. An ultrasound was booked at the early pregnancy unit the next day.

We arrived home feeling flat and worried. We cuddled up in bed and could do nothing but hope for the best. I was so nervous and dreading the scan.

The next day, I had an internal scan to assess the situation of the pregnancy. I was still bleeding.

I started crying even before sitting in the chair – I think I knew what was coming.

'I'm so sorry,' said the nurse, 'but this pregnancy has miscarried. There is no sign of an embryo here.'

There it was: our first miscarriage. We were devastated. As soon as we were out of the nurse's room, we stood there holding each other in inconsolable tears. It had been a long time since I'd felt so incredibly sad.

I had to phone mum the next morning to tell her – she was also devastated. My bleeding got heavier and heavier over the following days; it was miserable.

We hadn't had the chance to tell Trevor's parents the good news but decided to tell them about our loss; it was sad that they had not had a chance to experience happy news first, even for only a few days.

Chapter Five: Bella the Beagle

During this time Bonita the Border Collie gave us so much pleasure and helped lift our sorrow. The walks we'd take together and the fun and entertainment she provided made me determined finally to get the Beagle I'd wanted for years.

The way that I deal with sadness is to replace it with something to work towards. In this case, my focus became to get pregnant again as quickly as possible. I used this as a distraction, helping me to deal with or bury the pain. Getting our Beagle would also help distract me while bringing pleasure at the same time. And that she did!

We already had dog-friendly lives and I planned to be at home for a couple of months in-between finishing one job and starting another, so this was the perfect time. On Christmas Eve, we collected our new family addition, Bella the Beagle.

Bella had a bumpy start with Bonita who was used to being the princess, a position disrupted by this smaller and slightly cuter princess.

We had a couple of anxious moments when Bella went near Bonita's food, but after a few weeks everything settled and Bonita learned to tolerate having an adopted little sister. She was my new baby (and still is!) and over time Trevor fell in love with her too. We had some beautiful times with our dogs and even managed to drive them over to Switzerland for a Christmas holiday.

Chapter Six: Our Second Pregnancy

I had become pregnant so quickly after the coil was removed that we assumed it would happen again but months went by and before we knew it six months had passed. My age was worrying me but Trevor was convinced it would be OK and I needed to stop stressing. Easier said than done as the following months brought more challenges.

I started looking for a new job. I wanted to find something I was passionate about and went for interviews.
Some roles I turned down because they were not right, but eventually I found one I was thrilled about and was asked to start as soon as possible.

Around this time Trevor's nephew was diagnosed with cancer and not long after, Trevor's father was also diagnosed with cancer. Fortunately, both made it through.

Fifteen months after our miscarriage, and just as we began to accept that we weren't going to have children together, my period was late. I took a pregnancy test and was thrilled to see a BFP (BIG FAT POSITIVE)!

We were over the moon but also aware we were 'high risk'. We attended all our antenatal appointments with hope and excitement, but also trepidation.

No matter how much I tried to distract myself, it was impossible to stop having flashbacks to the miscarriage.

Trevor was asked shortly after to photograph The Oscars, in LA and I went along too after checking with the doctor it was safe, to take my mind off things and have something else on which to focus.

The following months were a blur of working full-time and being pregnant. My flat hadn't sold and its rent wasn't enough to cover my own, so savings were diminishing fast. But with Ellie at university and Joel deciding to stay with his father, the pressure was off to rent a larger place.

Trevor wanted us to live in his stunning riverside flat in Battersea, but it was partly used for his business and I wanted to stay with my parents and be looked after. I couldn't envisage carting doggy beds, shopping and baby car seats up and down 8 floors on a regular basis. What was playing on my mind most, was our need for a family home for our baby and dogs. Although house hunting together was exciting it was also stressful.

A few weeks later was our 12-week scan. I was very nervous and lay shivering as Trevor held my hand. We waited for what felt like an eternity.

"Here's your baby's heartbeat," said the nurse. "Everything looks good and baby is healthy." We were overwhelmed with relief and excitement.

"We've done it," I thought.

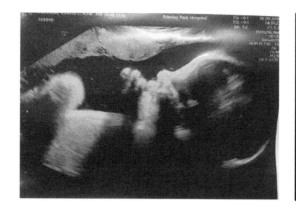

We managed to keep the pregnancy a secret – even from family – until after the 12-week scan.

Chapter Seven: Trevor's Mother Marion Dies

Along with the good news, came heartache. Marion, Trevor's mum, had one working lung for years and when that began to fail, she was admitted to hospital.

Trevor and I had been house hunting in Suffolk when we heard the news and rushed to be with her. She was in great spirits, but little did we know what was to come.

We decided to tell her our good news and she was delighted. It really gave her a boost we thought but then she deteriorated quickly, was to be sedated and put on a ventilator. Sadly, on 18th April 2018, she passed away.

I was at work when Trevor called me. He had stayed by her side for the last few days and could hardly speak from sobbing. I sat on the stairs of our office building – I must have looked crazy, a heavily pregnant woman on the stairs, crying with him on the phone.

Chapter Eight: It's a boy!

Commuting from my parents' house in Lightwater became harder and having Trevor, me, and the two dogs staying took its toll on my parents.

Trevor re-organised his business so his flat could be a living space and when we were ready, we continued with our house-hunt.

On 7th July, we had our sexing scan. I couldn't hazard a guess whether we were having a boy or a girl because I had been wrong with both Ellie and Joel so doubted my instincts.

We asked the nurse to write the baby's gender on a piece of paper instead of telling us so we could open it together at lunch. It was a boy!

Bobby was our nickname for bump because he kept bobbing around. He was very active throughout our relatively smooth pregnancy, so he became 'Bobby Baby Bump'. Then we progressed his nickname to 'Big Bobby Baby Bump' then towards 37 weeks, 'Bl**dy Big Bobby Baby Bump'!

Chapter Nine: We're Engaged!

Our house hunt took us to a place called Elmer where there was a partly sandy beach and on an afternoon stroll, on my 43rd birthday, after a family meal, Trevor unexpectedly dropped to one knee and proposed with a delicate ring that had belonged to his grandmother.

It felt as if things were finally coming together but we decided not to have the wedding until after the baby had arrived.

Chapter Ten: The Big Move

The months flew by and I was growing bigger and rounder. Life felt quite stressful as we still hadn't found a house to buy. At work, my company was being taken over so there was a lot of change and a lot to do.

Then, one night (I did a lot of house hunting during the nights when I couldn't sleep), something remarkable happened. I Google 'Sandy Beach South Coast' and a restaurant called *Billy's On The Beach* appeared not far from Elmer. It looked amazing and was dog friendly.

When we visited, the tide was out and there it was, our sandy beach! The weather was horrific that day, windy and raining, but we both knew this area was for us, more than Elmer and that we would be spending many more days on this beach.

One property stood out and was in our budget, about 10 minutes' drive from the beach, tucked away in a village called Sidlesham.

We put in a rental offer after a second viewing which was accepted just in time for our next antenatal appointment. Finally, we'd found ourselves a home.
It was renting rather than buying but was a fabulous compromise. The garden was perfect for the dogs and children to play in.

A few days later we had our next antenatal appointment. We were thrilled to see our baby again but our elation subsided when the consultant told us I had developed a condition called Polyhydramnios, an excess of amniotic fluid in the sac seen in about 1% of pregnancies, and a Caesarean section would be needed in case the umbilical cord got tangled around the baby.

We explained we were moving to Chichester, so he wrote a letter to our next consultant with details of the situation and advised us to book to see the new consultant immediately.
Leaving the hospital, we felt flat and worried. I had been hoping for natural labour but that choice had been taken from us.

Quickly we moved into our new home, and had an amazing couple of days. Joel came to help us unpack and we took him to Billy's restaurant for breakfast and showed him around. Joel put his head on my belly and could feel Bobby kick!

The following day, we went to our local hospital to 'check in' and drop off our paperwork with the previous consultant's letter. At least we knew where the hospital and labour ward was, as it was only a few weeks until my due date.

Our check-in appointment went well and our new consultant was reassuring. We listened to Bobby's strong heartbeat and were booked for our Caesarean in three weeks. I could hardly wait!

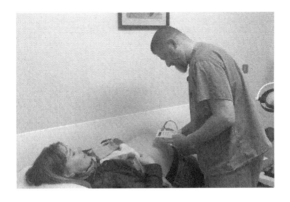

But only two days later, Bobby was kicking like crazy. I was in so much pain I shut myself in our bathroom and cried. Bella jumped up at me and looking back she must have been trying to tell me something was wrong. It felt as if Bobby was pulling at my belly button.

When I told Trevor, he suggested telling a nurse at our antenatal class that day and when I mentioned it to her, she said I might have a hernia, a common condition at this stage of pregnancy.

She suggested placing a thick sanitary towel over the area to protect it and soothe the pain. (I got to the bottom of this years later when it turned out she was right. I have a belly button hernia which pops out sometimes later in my pregnancies.)

The morning went quickly. It was great to meet other people, although the class went into detail about natural birth and what happens when you go into labour when I knew I was having a Caesarean. The last activity of the session taught the partners how to massage mum-to-be. Trevor massaged my tummy, which was so soothing.

That night, we made dinner and headed off to bed early. We had no idea the next day would be the worst of our lives.

PART THREE

Chapter Eleven: Baby Bobby's Heartbeat Stops

This day will forever be burned in our memories.

We left quite early in the morning that Sunday to get the cot and nursery furniture. We wandered around Ikea but were in a hurry as we were going to Petworth to see Father Peter about organising an annulment so that we could get married in a Catholic church.

"I can't feel Bobby moving as much today," I told Trevor when we got back to the car.

On the journey home, Trevor played Bruce Springsteen's *Drive All Night*.

"Would you like this to be our wedding song?"

"Of course, it's perfect babe," I replied.

Nothing was mentioned about my baby bump in our meeting with Father Peter. I hadn't felt Bobby move still – I assumed he must have worn himself out jumping around yesterday.

We had planned to walk the dogs after the meeting but I was concerned as we pulled into the car park. "I need to sit for a few moments, I still haven't felt Bobby kick," I said to Trevor.

"Do you want to stay here in the car while I walk the dogs?" he asked.

"No, I'd like to come. "I'm sure some fresh air will be good."

I took the climb easy, and while the view was worth it, I still felt something was not right. When we got home, I just wanted to rest. I stayed in bed all evening listening to the banging of our baby furniture being put together.

When I finally felt Bobby move, he was less energetic than normal and wasn't kicking.

At 3:30am I woke Trevor. "Babe, I'm getting worried. I haven't felt kicking and it's starting to scare me." We called the hospital and grabbed the bag I'd packed weeks ago, just in case. The nurse told us, "Try not to worry but come in so we can see what's happening."

The car park was empty when we arrived and I became nervous as we entered the building. After a urine sample, we were shown to the ward and a bed.

My heart still pounds, years on, thinking about what came next.

I was sent for a scan and the nurse said the terrible words, "I'm having an issue finding the heartbeat."

My heart crashed and I felt like passing out. The nurse went to get help.

We waited for what felt like an eternity but really was probably only minutes. Another nurse entered the room and explained that he had come to perform a second scan.

From the way he spoke, I suspected the worst.

The silence was deafening as Trevor gripped my clammy hands.

"I'm so sorry, so sorry," said the nurse. "There's no heartbeat. Your baby has died."

I can't remember much except our screams and sobbing. "I'm so sorry," I remember saying to Trevor over and over, the guilt overwhelming me.

I had lost our baby.

We had heard Bobby's strong heartbeat only a few days before.

'I've called your consultant," said the nurse. "He's on his way."

Our consultant, Jan, was devastated too. He explained what he had found and then left us for a while. All I remember of this moment now, was a blur of sobs and cries. Heartache and tears. Maybe screams. Maybe anger. Confusion. Why? Why Bobby? Why us? Where is his soul? Is it here with us in this room?

A while later, I've no idea how long, Jan came back to give his condolences and the next steps. A private room was being organised for us. He and his team were there to support us through the coming days.

He asked if we'd like to have one final scan. I just wanted to see his little body and hoped this was all some terrible mistake... but there was definitely no heartbeat. After leaving us for a short time, he returned with the terrible task of discussing next steps.

The next hours, days, weeks and months were, without a doubt, dark and the hardest of our lives. I'm not sure how we pulled through.

"Oh Christ, I have to give birth to our dead baby." The horror dawned on me.

"I can't! How can I do that?" I've never been so frightened. Giving birth to a live baby was frightening enough, but this? '*This must be a nightmare*, I kept telling myself.

I'll wake up soon.'

Chapter Twelve: Baby Bobby Born Sleeping

The consultant gave us terrible options – wait for a few days to be induced and give birth naturally or proceed the next day with a C-section. I think I was still numb.

Our precious little baby had died.

"You don't have to decide anything right now," he said.

"Perhaps go home and rest or go for a walk."

Through the haze we agreed – we needed time to catch our breath and tell our families. "You are going to be OK," he attempted to reassure us, but nothing on this earth could have reassured us at that moment.

The decision was a no brainer for me. I'd experienced both natural childbirth and a C-section and I was not going through natural birth for a baby who had died, nor was I going to put Trevor through it.

Enough was enough. A C-section it would be.

The options were horrific and terrifying, or more horrific and more terrifying. I could have a general anaesthetic and not see our baby which was initially the best option for me, I felt that by not seeing him the pain would be less.

Trevor wanted the chance to hold his son before we said goodbye but the thought terrified me. Bobby's soul had already left and I was scared I might crumble seeing his beautiful body empty and I would die from a broken heart. Part of me wanted to, but I trusted Trevor's feelings, something I've learned to do more over the years, and now, I'm so glad I did.

Those precious moments when we held Bobby fill me with warmth, not sadness. He deserved every second of those precious times and cuddles we had with him.

So, there was our answer; to have a C-section with an epidural so Trevor could be with us the whole way through.

I don't remember leaving the hospital still pregnant with my sleeping baby.

We went home to the dogs who helped us through our next hours, days, months, and years.

If you have doggies, you'll understand.

The first person to know was our neighbour who had signed for a delivery in our absence. It was a baby bath. He kept hold of it for us for a few weeks until we could face him handing it over to us. He was devastated for us and organised the neighbours to help with the dogs even though we were new to the area, a kindness for which we are still grateful.

"You're so brave," another neighbour said.

Am I? I wondered, or was I just numb and looking brave because it hadn't sunk in yet? Shock and bravery are not the same thing.

My parents were in Spain, so we had to call them. This was by far the worst thing I have ever had to tell my parents.

There was no way of preparing them or twisting it with any kind of positivity.

Mum broke down at the news and poor dad just looked so worried and said,

"I'm not sure how you're mentally going to get through this one, Karen."

Nor did I.

Mum wanted to get the next flight home but there was no point; we were going to be in hospital for a couple of days now.

Next, we told Trevor's father and step-mother. It was only six months since we'd lost Trevor's mum and now, Bobby.

They were both devastated.

Ellie and Joel were next.

Joel was on holiday in Amsterdam with his friends so I couldn't bring myself to tell him until he returned home. I called Ellie, she went into shock and my heart broke again.

At first, she didn't understand what I meant when I told her we had 'lost Bobby', so I explained what had happened with his heartbeat.

There was silence, followed by how sorry she was. "You will get through this mum," I remember her saying.

I will remember those final moments with Bobby inside me clearly for the rest of my life.

Trevor and I sat at the seaside at Billy's in the bracing wind, focusing on one thing at a time... such as whether we would like to name him.

We had previously decided on a name for our baby (it wasn't really Bobby). Archie would have been his name but part of me didn't want to use it because we already knew we were going to try again for a baby and what if it was a boy?

We could use the name next time.

"Babe, why don't we just keep his name as Bobby?" I said.

We both knew it made sense.

I was anxious to get the worst over. Terror doesn't come close to explaining how I felt about this next step. We packed essentials and headed back to the hospital. The room I was assigned was our sanctuary and prison for the next few days, where we would hold our sleeping baby and sob our hearts out.

I changed into a theatre gown, feeling exposed under the flimsy robe. One nurse, Inga, was our rock through the horror that was about to unfold.

Inga guided me into the theatre and the doctors slid the epidural into my spine. "Hold Trevor's hand and mine," she instructed. "Keep looking at me and squeeze my hand. We are going to get through this and you are going to be OK. Look in my eyes." My legs were numb from the epidural, but I could still feel a rocking sensation, like being put on a washing machine spin cycle.

I tried to stay focused on Inga through my tears. After what felt like an eternity the doctor said, "We have him."

And there he was, Bobby Preston Adams. The nurses wrapped him in a blanket and passed him to me. I held him tight, feeling the soft warmth of his skin. We both had him wrapped in our arms and we were howling, our hearts ripped to pieces. He looked perfect.

The feeling of loss and grief I'd felt before when I had lost grandparents, aunts and friends doesn't even touch the surface of the pain I felt. I understand fully now what a broken heart means.

I looked at his little lifeless face and stroked his cheek, wondering where his soul was right now. Had it gone to heaven already? Or was it in the room looking over us all, wondering what to do next? Did he feel our sadness? I really hoped not because I wouldn't want him to feel the pain we were in.

I gradually started to breathe again. Inga still held me and Trevor when we needed it until we were wheeled back to our room where Bobby was put in a cot next to us.
It began to hit me that we would never get to know him.
How cruel was this world taking our baby?

I felt as if I was in a sick film... this couldn't possibly be real. I was in a lot of pain from the C-section – it's a major operation and would take time to heal.
My heart probably never would.

Baby Bobby stayed with us all night. We were looked after by the nurses and there was constantly someone with us. They helped by talking if we wanted to talk or left us alone in the moments we needed space.
I lost track of time over the two days we spent in that room.

Joel arrived back in the country from his Amsterdam trip and I had to tell him.
"I have some bad news, son. We've lost Bobby."

"What do you mean, Mum?"

"His heart stopped, and he died darling."

"Mum, I'm so sorry," he said, his voice quivering.

We were asked if we wanted to dress Bobby.

Trevor wanted to do it and it was beautiful to watch him take such care.

He had put nappies on his nephew many years ago but never, of course, on his own baby. He put Bobby in his babygrow, did up the poppers, wrapped him in a blanket and put him back into his cot.

Although beautiful to watch, it was so, so wrong.

Why had the world done this to him? To us?

Watching him at that moment made me determined that one day he would be dressing his own living baby, so he could feel the joy that he should be feeling now.

Trevor wanted photos of Bobby. I both understood and was horrified but I watched him take them, while being held tight by a nurse as I sobbed uncontrollably.

I just wanted it to be over and to go home and be with Ellie and Joel.

We agreed for Bobby to have a post-mortem to understand what had happened and perhaps help save other babies.

When we left, the nurse helped us pack and gave us a beautiful memorial for bereaved parents, with handprints, a lock of Bobby's hair, a candle, and a book.
The book was called, 'Guess How Much I Love You'. I planned to keep this book for Bobby's brother or sister when we would have our rainbow baby.

I asked Trevor, "What are we going to do with Bobby's things? Can they fit in the loft?" "I don't want to put his things away," he replied.

That doesn't make any sense, I thought. I'm the type of person who prefers to put bad things or memories away to make way for new and good ones.

However, I have learned through this experience that relationships are about respect and understanding the other person's needs and we left Bobby's room as it was.

Ellie and Joel were at home when we arrived and I was so relieved to see them.
We spent the next couple of days, the four of us, cocooned in our grief but finding solace in each other.
I was still healing physically and slowly pulling my heart and mind back together.

More family and friends arrived when Ellie and Joel headed back to their worlds and the house was full of love and support.

One of my cousins sent me a book, *Ask Me His Name* by Elle Wright. The book helped me grieve for my own loss over the following weeks as it was about a couple who lost their baby, Teddy, a few days after birth.

It took six weeks from Bobby's birth to get the post-mortem results, after which we could book a funeral and say good-bye.

Our hospital counsellor explained that they could organise a funeral and we didn't need to attend, or we could organise our own; whatever we felt was right. I couldn't cope with organising a big funeral, so we opted for a small, immediate family-only funeral.

There were days when we could get up and head out, maybe for a walk, or to a supermarket and there were days when the grief was too much.
On those days, we'd curl up under the bed covers and not move.

I became focused on getting pregnant again which meant getting my body back on fertility diets, exercise, and yoga, had massages with an expert, Sally Cranfield, and booked sessions with an acupuncturist, Gill Bescoby.

Gill saved me during my period of grief, I don't know how she stayed so strong. I booked to see her once, maybe twice a week, and she advised me on my health and on trying to get pregnant again as quickly as possible. Her treatment room is a beautiful, peaceful log cabin near West Wittering, about 10 minutes' drive from our house.

Each visit she'd ask, "How are you?" There were days when I couldn't tell her because I'd burst into tears.
There were days when I felt stronger with just a bit of wobble.
No matter how bad I felt, she'd lay me on her magic bed, then pop (literally sometimes) needles all around my body, wherever they needed to be and let me rest for a while.

She was so good that I made sure Trevor went to visit her once a week too. His physical and mental health also needed to be in top shape, ready for our next conception.

Each time, by the end of the session, I'd feel renewed, strong again, ready to face the world. It would also refocus me on the hope of becoming pregnant again.

The irony is I hate needles!

We laugh about this now and I often ask her if she could re-qualify in something more pleasant like massage!

I also booked plenty of these for both of us. The week after we lost Bobby, I frantically searched for and found a masseuse who could visit the house (I couldn't drive after having the C-section). Sally Cranfield, or Sally Massage as I call her, started coming regularly as part of our fertility preparation and health support.

I am a fan of massage and firmly believe it is a preventative treatment but also vital for good physical and mental health.

Chapter Thirteen: Baby Bobby's Funeral.

Organising Bobby's funeral was like being stuck in another nightmare.

We should have been organising his christening, not his funeral.

Where do you even start organising your baby's funeral?

I couldn't cope with a big funeral. I'm Irish Catholic and usually a funeral would be a big event, almost a party to celebrate the deceased's life. But for Bobby there was no life to celebrate and as amazing as my family are, I couldn't face lots of people at this time. My heart was in too many pieces.

Being new to the area we didn't know where our nearest Catholic church was. We found one in East Wittering, St Peters. The funeral would be held there and because we already had a relationship with Fr Peter from Petworth, we asked him if he could do the service.

There would be a short church service and then Bobby would be cremated at Chichester crematorium. A landmark which still, and always will fill me with dread.

At the funeral parlour, the lady who helped us had been through a similar experience herself many years ago and understood how we felt.

She helped us make dreadful decisions such as choosing the coffin and at the end of our appointment I was given a piece of paper giving permission for baby Bobby's body to be cremated.

As I was signing, the tears were soaking the page and I never thought I'd ever be able to sign anything with my signature ever again.

We then had to choose the music we wanted. During the run-up to the funeral, I had been listening to the song *Chasing Cars* by Snow Patrol. The song evoked images of myself with baby Bobby, the two of us lying together playing with cars, just wasting time and having fun.

That's what we should have been doing. Why had this chance been taken away from us?

So, from that moment, Chasing Cars became my song for Bobby. Still when I hear it, I either let myself cry or try to control my emotions by breathing slowly.

When I suggested having this song for the funeral Trevor didn't really get it. It's taken a while but a few years on, I think he does now.

We listened to many other songs, trying to decide which to have. All of them broke our hearts but eventually we went with Eric Clapton, *Tears in Heaven*. Of course, anytime we hear this song now we look at each other, take a deep breath and work through the moment, or one of us cries, which sets off the other one and we cry our way through the song. I'm sure this will never stop. And you know what? That's OK.

The day of the funeral was a blur. Ellie and Joel decided not to attend, which I felt torn about but respected their decision, so there were only ten of us at the church, immediate family members only.

We brought Trevor a new shirt and I wore an old favourite black dress. I wasn't sure we were actually going to be able to make it through a day that saw both of us start in tears and I was drinking red wine while I dressed.

A fundraiser page we had launched for Chichester hospital was a small ray of light in the darkness. When we hit £3,000 as we left for the funeral, it gave us a boost that at least there was something beautiful about today.

But then the car arrived and my heart sank. Our baby Bobby's tiny coffin was in that car.

318%

£3,180

raised of £1,000 target by 89 supporters

Share

Karen
Preston

We've raised £3,180 to support the wonderful team in the maternity ward at St Richard's Hospital in Chichester who helped us through the worst moment imaginable.

Don't have time to donate right now?
Set up a reminder

In memory · Funded on Friday, 1st March 2019

Our nurse, Inga, who had helped us through baby Bobby's birth, was there and as we walked down the aisle of the church, I found myself launching at her for a hug and Trevor wrapped his arms around both of us.

"You can do this," she whispered and squeezed us both hard.

A lady I had not met before gave a reading. I later found out her name was Gill and years before she had lost a baby. She'd heard what had happened and wanted to help.

I don't remember most of the service; I think I may have blocked some of it out as it was so painful. I thought again,

"Why us? Why Bobby? Where is his soul now?"

The thought of his tiny body going through the cremation chamber was too much to bear. I needed the day to be over.

After the service, we all went for a meal at a local restaurant which distracted us for the night, but the day after the funeral we both felt empty. Everybody tried hard to comfort and support us but I fell into a black hole.

There had been the waiting and build-up to the funeral and now, nothing.

PART FOUR

Chapter Fourteen: Slow Steps to Recovery

It took a couple of months, but I gradually started to see people again and do 'normal' things like go shopping at the supermarket. As part of my recovery, I found the determination to refocus on fertility and another baby.

We had no idea that we still had a huge journey ahead of us.

We also had to allow ourselves to grieve for Bobby.

This grief will never go away, it runs so deep.

You sometimes hear people say they'll never be the same after a tragedy and now I understand in a way I never could before.

I had to be patient with myself when I got emotional. It catches you when you're least expecting it. Sometimes, I'd find myself sobbing while walking around, like when I accidentally stumbled on the baby aisle in John Lewis.

I felt so much pain as I yearned to feed and hold my baby.

I don't think these moments will ever stop. They can be triggered by the most random situations. It is just part of grieving for my baby and I have learned to allow myself these moments - they have become my special moments for me and Bobby.

Bobby's Post-Mortem

Another step in our grieving process was to make any sense of what had happened and attend an appointment with our consultant, Jan to discuss Bobby's post-mortem.

Basically, it had been discovered that the placenta had stopped providing for Bobby with no obvious cause or reason and there wasn't enough oxygen getting to him.

It wasn't much of an explanation, and it was impossible not to analyse my every move throughout my pregnancy and not blame myself.

With a glimmer of positivity, Jan told us that if we had a future pregnancy, I would be given blood thinning injections to help with the provision to the placenta and that I would be very closely monitored and screened.

This news just made me more and more determined to get pregnant again. As soon as possible.

Exercise is key for me, for both my mental and physical health. I don't really like running but I love the feeling afterwards in the shower. I rebuilt my fitness and started running four miles a day. Trevor and I both continued with acupuncture, had regular massages, and followed fertility diets attempting to control the variables.

Every month that my period arrived had me in tears.

I also cried a lot in the run-up to Christmas, which should have been Bobby's first.

There will always be a hole in my heart where Bobby should be.

In January, I returned to work. The company I had been working for had been taken over and I had a new line manager who became an amazing mentor and friend. The Human Resources team agreed that I could work from home three days a week and travel to London for the other two.

My life became busy again. As months passed, and there was still no pregnancy, going to work became my lifeline. It made me get up in the mornings and gave me something else to think about other than Bobby and the desperation we felt to fall pregnant again.

Chapter Fifteen: Our IVF Journey Begins

By May I was yearning to try IVF, but Trevor's friend had recently gone through IVF, so far without success, and had been finding it an exhausting and expensive journey which gave Trevor reservations about going down this road.

He was convinced we should conceive naturally, but after months of no success he finally agreed to an initial meeting. The first step was to find out what was involved, so I attended an open evening run by a local fertility clinic.

The presenting doctor clearly knew the finer details of IVF and I instantly trusted him. We decided to visit their Portsmouth clinic but they had limited availability and were slow to reply.
So many things went wrong with this clinic that it got to the point where I wouldn't trust them to make a cup of tea, never mind help us with medical support to create a baby!

Firstly, there was a mix-up with the appointment, and we were sent to the wrong consultant; next their portal wouldn't work for Trevor when he was adding his personal details. It was good, however, to speak to the doctor at our appointment.
Once women turn 40, their eggs start to run out and testing showed that my AMH level (egg availability) was very low. While I had been very aware of my age being a problem, Trevor hadn't

and presumed it would be easy, so I was glad when the doctor explained that the chance of us conceiving naturally was incredibly small.

I hugged Trevor as he absorbed the information and thought, *this shouldn't be so bloody hard*!

Another mistake of the clinic was that despite Trevor driving to Southampton (an hour away) the day before, the sperm test results hadn't been received in time for our meeting, so we had to continue with the appointment on the assumption that the results were all OK. The outcome was that even with IVF it was going to be hard for us to conceive... but we could try.

We decided to give it a go and notified the clinic that we wanted to start treatment as soon as we physically could, pending the semen results.

Before we even got the results, the payment chasing started. Email after email arrived, followed by phone calls. We still didn't have the semen results, so how could we proceed unless we were sure that was all OK?

Next, Trevor's results weren't ready when we were told they would be, and then he was given incorrect results. It really was a disaster.

We lost faith in the clinic and needed to decide whether to proceed but because we were feeling as though we were running out of time, we continued. I would start hormone injections on Friday 31st May 2019.

On the day we were due to start, I phoned Trevor and asked him to get a pregnancy test on the way home to be sure I wasn't pregnant before we started.

Well would you believe it, I took the test and miraculously, we got a positive line!

We called the emergency number for the fertility clinic and went first thing on Saturday morning for a blood test which showed positive HCG levels 11.5 - good news!

We were advised to go back on Wednesday to check that levels were rising. The results were due on Thursday morning but they weren't available when we called. Trevor followed up, and the nurse said she'd chase and call back.

Half an hour later the nurse called Trevor informing him that the new level was 250 and explained that after an initial reading of 11.5, she'd expected to see the levels double every 24 hours and this level had more than exceeded that. It was good news - I was very definitely pregnant.

We were over the moon; we'd done it!

No need for IVF injections – hooray!

The next morning Trevor left early and I was enjoying a lie-in but woke to my phone ringing. Who would call me at this time on a Saturday?

It was the nurse from the clinic, who without ceremony said, "I'm sorry, I'm not sure what's happened. Your results show a lower level than we thought and if the levels keep going down this isn't likely to be an ongoing pregnancy."

Our world tipped upside down again and devastation hit. I barely moved from bed for days. I had more blood tests done through my own doctor and as advised the pregnancy was not on-going.

We received an email apology from the clinic which explained we had **been given somebody else's results.**

That was it; we reported the clinic to a governing body and demanded our money back.

Finally, on 5th August 2019, we had some good news. We had both received annulments from the Pope to say our marriages had been formally ended and we now had permission to marry in a Catholic church.

We were able to set our wedding date at long last. We decided on the 19th September 2020 and started wedding planning, with no idea what 2020 would bring.

Chapter Sixteen: Discovering an Ovarian Cyst

I began exploring clinics abroad and stumbled upon one called Team Miracle, based in Nicosia, Northern Cyprus (Northern Cyprus is Turkish). I messaged them and explained our story to an incredibly responsive lady. Prices for IVF appeared to be so much lower than in the UK, so it was tempting to jump in, but we decided to try one more clinic close to home first.

The price difference between having IVF in Cyprus and having IVF in the UK is substantial. It can be tricky doing a like for like comparison and there are lots of items / services that can be added on to basic packages, but basically, for straight forward IVF in the UK (pre-checks, egg & sperm collection and embryo implantation) it costs around £6,000 and in Cyprus, this basic package starts at around £3,500.

What was so appealing to us was that for less money than you would spend on IVF at home, you could have a really good holiday included, with the added appeal that you don't have to juggle medical appointments around work, meaning you are far more relaxed. In addition, Cyprus is known as the 'Island of Love' and I now understand why!

There are many additional options available which can bump up the price massively; we tried some of the extras on some cycles and not on others.

The next clinic we tried was also based in Southampton. After an initial consultation, the doctor we spoke to recommended IUI (Intra-Uterine Insemination) which is a little bit different from IVF, less intrusive and less expensive, so we agreed to give it a go.
We were excited to try this method and arranged a meeting with the consultant to proceed but first we needed a womb thickness scan before starting medication. I was starting to regain hope and felt as if we were starting to get somewhere.

We arrived at the clinic ready for our scan, a little anxious but excited to move forward. We had a pre-scan meeting with a nurse and more issues with paperwork (they'd sent me the incorrect documents to complete prior to the appointment, so we had to do them all over again).

Having scans at this stage was traumatic because I would get flashbacks of the loss of Bobby's heartbeat so I had to take slow, deep breaths to avoid a panic attack.
"Is everything OK?" I asked the nurse when her face creased while staring at the monitor. "I'm not sure," she replied. "I can see a cyst on your ovary. This is very common and I'm sure it's

nothing to worry about. But we may have to wait a while before we continue to allow the cyst to shrink."

I almost couldn't believe it and my heart sank at yet another challenge.

"How long is this all going to take?" I wondered.

I immediately called my GP, who advised me to call our nearest private hospital (thankfully I had private health insurance through work) and booked an appointment. Within a few days, I had an appointment with a consultant, Ms Melanie Tipples.

I fought back tears when explaining our journey.

Within a week, Ms Tipples had me in for surgery to remove the cyst and have a womb scrape to help with conception.

We decided to bin the IUI idea entirely and to head to Northern Cyprus, to Team Miracle, for IVF. Team Miracle was the only company I had faith in after every incompetence of those in the UK. And to be honest, we really needed a holiday.

Chapter Seventeen: Our Fourth Pregnancy

Nicole, the co-ordinator at the clinic in Cyprus, helped us to finalise our IVF plans and sent us the required medications. When they arrived, the boxes completely covered our kitchen table and I marvelled at how much was meant to go into my body.

There was no way I could inject myself – the thought made me feel sick, so the task fell to Trevor who learned to mix and administer the injections. Now I had my very own Dr Trevor Adams!

We did break more than one glass vial, but we (Trevor) got used to it eventually.

I had up to three daily injections at a time and my poor tummy was covered in bruises.

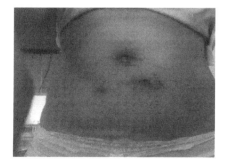

Nicole gave us the IVF medication and menstrual cycle timings so we could book flights. We planned to stay in Cyprus for ten days in September; we would have the sperm and egg collection on day two of our stay and then embryo transfer five days later.

Our injections had to be taken at certain times every day and we were due one as soon as we landed at Larnaca airport.
I half expected us to get arrested as we locked ourselves in a disabled toilet to mix the drugs and administer the injections.
We realised we were short of some of the medicine, so I messaged the clinic team at 4am and within half an hour we had a reply saying,
"Don't worry, we'll deliver what you need to the hotel reception in the morning," and that's what happened, a very different service from what we'd received in the UK.

We arrived at our hotel expecting something glamorous but the hotel was basic.
We asked to change rooms but the upgrade wasn't much better so we decided to make the most of it by stocking up on candles to make the apartment ambient and homely.

The following morning, we were scheduled for egg and sperm retrieval at the clinic. We were welcomed by a man called Hakan. He would be the person to look after us and go over all the arrangements, give information, and also take payment.

Hakan was friendly and explained the procedure in detail and answered our many questions. We then went into the doctor's room for our consultation and a scan.

The scanning room was small. Two nurses came in with us to watch, speaking to each other in Turkish while we waited for the doctor. I got myself up onto the 'glamour chair' feeling a little nervous but very excited.

The doctor introduced himself. He was friendly but stern and clearly an expert.

As he was scanning, he shook his head; it didn't look good.

He spoke to the nurses and then asked me to get dressed again and meet him in his office. I looked at Trevor – he was worried and pale. I started feeling very nervous and thought, "Oh, what now?"

The nurse stayed with me until I was dressed and guided Trevor and me into the doctor's office, where Hakan joined us.

'OK, I have examined your womb", he said, "and unfortunately we cannot perform your embryo transfer today because you have ovulated. You are going to need to come back again next month or the month after."

We can freeze the embryos today and they will still be OK – in fact sometimes the success rates are higher using frozen embryos.

Do you have any questions?"

I felt sick with disappointment. We still had another week booked in Cyprus – what a waste of holiday and money!

I gathered my thoughts and decided to turn this into a positive.

"Babe, let's just enjoy our holiday and each other. We're here now, there's no point buying more flights home. Let's just have some fun.

And then, to be honest, what's the hardship of coming back again to beautiful Cyprus and having a lovely weekend break in November?"

So that's what we did and I'm so glad because we were able to truly relax and enjoy each other.

We took boat trips, tours around the ghost town of Famagusta, went to casinos, and scuba dive.

Best of all, it reminded us of why we fell in love in the first place.

When we went home, I redoubled my efforts to prepare my body by following fertility recipes, no coffee, no alcohol, early nights, massages, acupuncture, and everything else possible. We booked our trip for the embryo transfer on November 19th.
I would be 42 and three months.

We visited Ms Tipples for a womb thickness scan and this time it was perfect.
Ms Tipples would also be handling our aftercare along with our consultant from St Richard's Hospital when we got a positive result.

Nicole messaged us just before our flight back to Cyprus, informing us of the time we were expected at the clinic the following morning.
We were really pleased with our hotel this time. It was out of holiday season, so a higher star place was affordable. We unpacked and headed to the harbour for dinner, ready for an early start in the morning.

In the back of my mind, I couldn't help but wonder what could go wrong this time.
We arrived at the clinic feeling nervous, but this time the scan was perfect.

I had requested acupuncture before and after embryo transfer as it can increase the success of IVF by 65%.

When we were taken to a room, I lit little tea light candles.
In my mind, I thought of Bobby's spirit coming back to us, with the candles acting as a guide so Bobby knew where to go (of course I didn't mention this to anybody else!). I was still convinced that baby Bobby's soul would come back in another baby's body.
Am I crazy for thinking this?
Maybe, maybe not. But I'm not sure that thought will ever really go away.

A nurse came to take me to the surgery room. I tried to explain to the nurses that Trevor wanted to come with me to see the embryo transfer but they didn't speak English and had no idea what I was trying to say. I could feel myself starting to panic.
"I need to speak to the doctor," I said. "He can't miss this!"
"We will ask the doctor when we go down," the nurse replied in broken English.

By the time the doctor arrived, I was in floods of tears, partly because I wanted Trevor to be with me and to see this but partly because he must have been panicking about not being there and worrying about me too.

"Trevor has been next to me every step of the way and I can't even imagine doing this without him being here," I explained to the doctor, tears streaming. I felt like a spoiled child but couldn't help it.

"OK, we're going to go and get him," said the doctor, "but he must not film or take photos."

"Of course," I agreed. I was so relieved when Trevor arrived in his scrubs.

Now I was ready.

We watched the ultrasound screen in silence and he held my hand as the tube was inserted into my womb.

The mood in the room was tense – we held our breath throughout the procedure which took no longer than two minutes and that was that. Done.

I was carefully lifted onto another bed before being wheeled back to my room to rest.

"Congratulations on your pregnancy!" said Hakan.

"You are now pregnant until proven otherwise." He went through our questions, advice on dos and don'ts, and told us that the team would be on standby to support us.

To this day, I feel the clinic's support is second to none.

I was given another round of acupuncture and asked Trevor to light the candles again. I prayed with all my heart that this would work.

We headed back to Kyrenia and treated ourselves to a lovely lunch and I walked around slowly and with care. Afterwards, we went back to our beautiful hotel, snuggled up on the bed and watched Netflix. For the next few days of our stay, we took things very slowly before returning home for the "two-week wait".

Back in England, it wasn't as hard as I had expected as I was able to work from home which provided a great distraction. We were advised not to use home tests (that was a bit of relief as I'd been torturing myself with them all year) as the clinic wanted HCG levels which could only be established from a blood test.
My doctor arranged a blood test at our local hospital and after a long day of waiting, I called the surgery to find out the result.
We were overwhelmed when the result was positive!

With the usual pregnancy symptoms, I needed to take things easy and wait for the heartbeat scan in a few weeks.
Then one morning, about a week later, I woke up and my breasts were not sensitive like they had been. I called the hospital who advised me to stay calm until the scan, but three weeks felt like a long, long wait.

When it finally came around, my heart was in my throat. Our consultant was the same consultant who had overseen all our issues with Bobby and also his post-mortem, Jan. He must have been hoping this would work for us.

But he was quiet as he scanned.

"It's not quite what I would have liked to see," he said finally.
"We might be too early but we should have another blood test to make sure your HCG levels are still rising. I'm so sorry to not have better news."

We had the blood test done immediately and the consultant called us that evening with bad news. HCG levels had decreased and the pregnancy was not progressing.

I could either wait for a miscarriage or go for a Dilation and Curettage procedure (D&C), which clears the uterine lining after a miscarriage.

Trevor had popped out to the shop as the consultant called me back.

When he walked through the door I burst into tears. Our hearts sank all over again.

I decided to have the D&C and the following day I was back at the hospital. I had a few days for recovery and when I felt better, I messaged Nicole at Team Miracle.

"When can we try again?" I asked, immediately focused on our next attempt. Giving up simply wasn't an option and the sooner we got back to Cyprus the better.

Chapter Eighteen: Our Fifth Pregnancy.

What kept us going after yet another devastating loss? Determination mostly, to keep trying until our time ran out. We so desperately wanted our own child or children together and there was still a part of me, crazy or not, that thought that Bobby's spirit and soul was watching over us, just waiting to come back but in another form and I needed to make it happen for him.

Two months later, Nicole ordered my medication again and we restarted the process. I focused on my health, what I ate, yoga, and exercise.

Soon we were off to Cyprus again, where we had embryos waiting in the freezer, our 'Freezer Geezers' as Trevor called them, so we would go for the transfer and then rest for a few days. This time around everything was familiar, including the hotel with the great food.

Nicole messaged us to be at the clinic for 9am and once again I had booked acupuncture before and after embryo transfer. The doctor allowed Trevor in the room so, for the second time, we could both watch the embryos being inserted into my womb. I had three implanted and chose to freeze the last three.

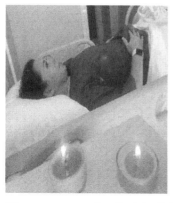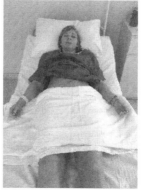

"Are you ready, Bobby? You can bring a brother or sister if you want to!" I thought.

Twins would be perfect!

After the procedure, we were hungry and headed out for lunch at a recommended restaurant across the road from the clinic. While we were sitting and drinking in the warmth, the most incredible rainbow I've ever seen appeared! Trevor rushed outside to take a photo.

"I know you're here, Bobby. I can't wait for you to be with us again."

Again, we rested at the hotel and enjoyed our time. It was very windy and there were few tourists as it was out of season during the winter, but it was a lovely break and we made the most of it.

Two weeks later, it was finally testing day and we went for the pregnancy blood test at St Richard's Hospital in Chichester.
When I called the doctor's surgery for the results, the doctor seemed confused. "So, you had a progesterone test done?" she asked. "No, a pregnancy test."
"I'm sorry, I think the wrong test has been done. I can't tell if you are pregnant from this test."

"But if I don't get the results tomorrow, we will have to wait all weekend!" I blurted out. My heart was thumping with anxiety, something I'd been warned to avoid. I needed to stay calm.

"OK, I'll create you a new test slip; can you collect it and go straight to the hospital?" Off I went without delay, and would you believe it? We got a positive result the second time around!
Good old Team Miracle!
And good old us; we did it!

Days went by and I started to feel confident about the pregnancy so we told family and friends but it was hard not to worry.
I tried not to complain or lose my cool with anybody but I got sick of people telling me not to worry. There are some who would gently say it, but others almost ordered it, as if I could control worry, flicking it as if it were a light switch.
Those people made me want to scream IF YOU'D GIVEN BIRTH TO YOUR DEAD BABY BY C-SECTION, HAD THREE MISCARRIAGES, 2 D&C OPERATIONS, GOD KNOWS HOW MANY INJECTIONS AND DRUGS THEN MAYBE, JUST MAYBE, YOU'D WORRY TOO!" But instead, I'd smile calmly or ignore them.

I made an appointment to see my GP the following day to discuss next steps. I was signed off work for two weeks to take things easy.

During the pregnancies following the loss of Bobby, I read a story to our baby every day; it was from the book 'Guess How Much I Love You' which had been given to us by the hospital as part of the gift box we left with. The trouble was, I just could never get past halfway, and I was in tears because I wanted to be reading it to baby Bobby too.

A week later, I woke in the middle of the night bursting for the toilet and when I looked down at the pan there was bright red blood. I freaked out.
Trevor tried to calm me. We lay in bed and for hours I Google until the bleeding stopped, hoping that the one bleed didn't mean a miscarriage.

I called the early pregnancy unit who said they couldn't scan until the following week, five days away!

We went to A&E instead, there was no scan available but a urine test gave me a positive result. We would have to sit tight until we could get the scan, for five torturous days.

I was physically shaking by the time of our appointment.
This time our consultant was on holiday and we had an Irish lady instead. I love the Irish and I love our hospital but I just didn't take to her. She was so blunt and, well, she just wasn't Jan.

The screen showed us two sacks but they were both empty. Either I had miscarried or the scan was too early and the heartbeats were not visible. "You'll need to come back in 10 days," said the nurse in a less than compassionate tone. "No way," I thought. "Another ten-day torturous wait"

We emailed our consultant, Jan, who arranged for us to see him on the tenth day.
We hoped for good news.

As we waited to go in, I said to Trevor:
"I wonder if Jan is nervous too. We've really put him through his paces, haven't we?"
It was a relief to see him. He's such a lovely man and he cares so much – his dedication was second to none and I'll always remember how amazing he was.

We made light conversation with the nurse while I positioned myself in the glamour chair. He scanned my tummy and a few moments later, he said,
"I'm so sorry guys but this just isn't a viable pregnancy. By now we should see the embryo."
I'd prepared myself for this but still his words shot through me and I could see it written on Trevor's face.
I decided in that moment that we wouldn't tell anybody about future pregnancies until we reached 12 weeks at least.

After yet another blow I couldn't go straight back to work, even from home. I emailed my boss to let him know what had happened. Again.

"Karen, I honestly don't know what to say. Please take as much time as you need, we will support you," was the reply I received. The support of my colleagues could never be measured but will always be appreciated. Thank you, thank you.

PART FIVE

Chapter Nineteen – IVF During Covid - 19

Just as we were recovering from our latest disappointment, within days in fact, we were hit with Covid-19. I could write a book on its own about this cycle!

Little did we realise how symbolic the rainbow would become, not just for us but for the whole world.

The virus hit Italy and Spain before the UK. Hundreds of thousands of people were dying and the health services couldn't cope. There was not enough protective equipment and medics had never seen anything quite like it.

Within weeks, the entire country was in lockdown. This meant that EVERYBODY (apart from key workers; doctors, care workers etc.) had to stay at home.

We were allowed out for one hour of exercise per day and couldn't go near anyone outside our own household.

The world went into hibernation. For me reality hit when Ellie and Joel couldn't come for Mother's Day. After everything, I'd been looking forward to spending that weekend with my family and it was taken away. I cried more about that than I had about our last miscarriage.

Sadly, the worst of this situation was still to come.

Covid-19 demanded isolation for the whole world.

Travel forbidden, flights cancelled, over 70s and people with underlying health issues forbidden to leave their houses for fear of catching the deadly virus.

Its arrival coincided with our IVF cycle, so to get through I was dedicated to my fitness regime.

My body needed to be in perfect condition for our next cycle, which I feared would be our last chance.

NHS workers fought to contain the virus and extra hospitals were set up in places like the Excel building in London. The whole country applauded the frontline workers outside on a Thursday evening at 8pm and each time I would cry, attempting to comprehend the unity caused by such tragedy.

The rainbow became the symbol of hope and people started putting rainbows in their windows, in signs on streets, in logos; there were rainbows everywhere.

Chapter Twenty – Travelling during Covid-19

The pandemic affected our IVF plans as most countries closed their borders for the first few months of the crisis. We had our final three embryos waiting for us in Northern Cyprus, which we were eager to return to, but we had to wait for three months after the last miscarriage.

Surely by June the pandemic would be under control?

Throughout, I had been in regular contact with Team Miracle; Nicole was a superstar – not only did she have many couples (and hormonal women) desperate to proceed but she had to work out their medication as normal, answer crazy questions including when the borders would reopen, all while carrying on with each woman's cycle schedule.

She has the patience of a saint!

It was July before the Northern Cyprus government released a list of countries which had to quarantine for 14 nights upon arrival and we were on it.

We were hoping that quarantine would be lifted by August as it was not an option for us.

Our final embryos were stuck in Northern Cyprus and Covid-19 was stopping us from getting them. What else could get in our way?!

The republic of Cyprus lifted the quarantine requirement from mid-July but that did not apply to Northern Cyprus which is classified as a different country from the South and I was losing hope. I had already started the medication so I was pumped with hormones.

Some countries were already going into second lockdowns and it was feared the UK would have a spike as autumn and winter approached.

I would be 44 in August and our final opportunity was being taken from us.

Then one day it was announced by the republic of Cyprus, that if a Covid test was taken no more than 72 hours before entry from countries other than the UK, quarantine wouldn't be required. We were thrilled and made plans.

Then came another bombshell – there would be redundancies in our department at work. I decided to take voluntary redundancy so that I could focus on my body and our final go at IVF. The redundancy was a small matter compared with our little Freezer Geezers waiting for us, but still...

I started looking into flights and accommodation via Turkey to avoid quarantine but the trip was getting complicated as timings had to coincide with the pill plan and the Covid test, while also keeping to a tight budget.

But we stayed positive through everything – we couldn't have seen any more rainbows than we had over the past six months and each one reminded me there was hope.

It was strange travelling amid Covid rules. Everybody wore masks in airports and there were queues to get into the terminal at Heathrow as people entering were kept to a minimum but our journey to Turkey was smooth and without hiccup.

A few days before our flight from Turkey to north-eastern Cyprus, I had to ramp up my medicines and start injections to ensure we would be on schedule for our arrival.
But the fear started. What would happen if something went wrong and we weren't allowed in?
Or we'd missed something? I shuddered at the thought.
We were scheduled for embryo transfer the following day so there was no space for even the smallest error.

Thankfully, everything went fine.
"And breathe", I repeated to myself. "We're coming little embryos - we're on our way to get you."

Chapter Twenty - One: Our Sixth Pregnancy:

Our embryo transfer was set for 14th August 2020, four days before my 44th birthday. We were familiar with the process and I fully trusted the team at the clinic.

As I'd done both times previously, I had acupuncture and this time we were going to try something different: using embryo glue. It was £500 extra but as this was the last chance it was worth a shot.
This was the third time we'd watched the embryo transfer on the screen and both Trevor and I were full of hope.

The return journey went smoothly and we would arrive home the day before my 44th birthday after an overnight stay in Turkey. On arrival in Turkey we waited for our luggage but the bags did not appear, including the bags of my medicine.

We spent over two hours waiting as airport staff searched – they found our other two bags but the third containing my medicine had vanished. There was nothing to be done except head to the hotel for the night.

The next morning Trevor tried so hard to make my birthday morning special but all I could think about was my medications and how my body needed them to hold the pregnancy, if there was one.

We headed back to the airport where no one was taking our predicament seriously. I lost it and yelled, "I'll have to find an IVF clinic in Istanbul for replacement medicines!"

It was the right thing to say, because as we'd checked in for the flight and our luggage was already loaded, the plane could only legally take off if I was on it! Otherwise, my luggage had to be found and removed.

Miraculously, it spurred the airport staff to find my missing case within half an hour. I quickly took my medications and within minutes all was well again.

We could finally relax and take our flight home.

I only had one week of work left when we returned, so I was winding down and handing over which allowed me to listen to my body, which I struggled to do when working.

The two-week wait didn't seem too long this time. We took the test and again it was good news. But the doctor cautioned that given my history I should

"Keep things calm and have another test in two days' time."
That's exactly what we did.

Although I knew the results from the doctor, I couldn't resist taking home tests. After we'd got the initial positive, I took one every day for about a week - it was such a joy to see that second line!

The second test at the doctors was also good news: the pregnancy was progressing!

I continued taking things easy, enjoying my redundancy, lunching with family and friends, applying for jobs and yes, writing this book! I had time to do things in the garden, snuggle up with Bella, and have afternoon naps.
care.
It was all going to be worth it.

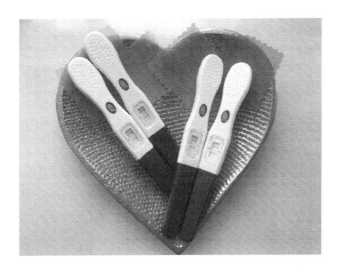

The medicines continued - my belly and my hips were like pincushions and my belly got so bruised, but I didn't care. It was all going to be worth it.

When we went for the first scan, Jan happily exclaimed,

"We've got a heartbeat!" The consultant was as delighted as we were.

I was clutching Trevor's hand as this incredible news blew our minds but I was also fearful. It was still early days (I was seven weeks pregnant by this time) and we had such a long way to go.

"OK," he said. "Given everything you've been through, this is clearly going to be a worrying pregnancy. What can we do to help?"

"Regular scans?" I asked.

"OK, let's get the next one booked. How about booking in two weeks?"

"Perfect, thank you," I said, feeling very cared for.

There were a few dramas over the next few weeks, including running low on meds that were nearly impossible to get in the UK. I called every chemist in the area, the doctors and local IVF clinics but nobody could help.

In the end, Team Miracle's supplier in Nottingham was able to help. This pharmacist is one of the most helpful people I have ever come across, offering a service second to none. Over the years, he has helped ensure we've received medicines on time at very short notice.

The delivery timing was too close for comfort - I had to take this injection at the same time early in the morning every day and the delivery wasn't due until lunchtime.

To compensate, I took a pessary of progesterone to keep the levels up.

One night, I awoke with stomach pains and was terrified.

"Here we go again," I thought. The pain got so bad I couldn't even stand up, so we called 111 for advice.

By the end of the conversation, the medic on the other end said, "Ok we have an ambulance on the way to you and it should be with you within 20 minutes." Within a few minutes the doorbell rang.

The paramedics carried out some basic checks, then gave me the choice of going to the hospital with them or with Trevor.

I chose the latter.

When I arrived at the hospital, Trevor wasn't allowed in due to Covid restrictions but a doctor from the maternity ward came to see me swiftly.

By then the pain had subsided and I just felt bruised.

We went through the symptoms, and it was decided that the problem was likely to do with digestion or constipation. I was embarrassed and was discharged, but within half an hour the doctor I'd just seen called my mobile. Our consultant, Jan wanted me scanned, so we went back to the hospital, our hearts thumping.

There was still a heartbeat! What a relief.
So that was an extra unexpected scan, only one week after the last one but Jan advised us to keep the scan appointment for the following week.

There were no dramas over the coming week and again, the next scan showed everything was normal and good. I started to really feel pregnancy symptoms; nausea, tiredness and tender breasts, which despite how it sounds, were all reassuring that we were on the right road.

At around 11 weeks, we booked the usual 12-week check. This is the scan when most people would hear their baby's heartbeat for the first time. It really started to feel like we were getting past the danger zone.
It was a massive relief.

I had decided to do things as differently as I could through this pregnancy, with the hope that it might help me hold onto it. I didn't even attempt to read *Guess How Much I Love You* this time. I thought that maybe in previous pregnancies it was creating stress inside.

There would be plenty of opportunities to read to our baby once we were holding him or her in our arms.

Chapter Twenty - Two: Pregnancy During Covid -19

Gradually the appointments came by post. One for the next routine scan, one for the specialist scan, and then the local midwife – Fran – called me to arrange a booking-in appointment. We already knew Fran because she had visited us every couple of days after we'd lost Bobby to check on us and ensure my C-section was healing.

I was starting to feel hopeful but still there was fear.

Because of the placenta issue when we lost Bobby, an extra scan was carried out with a specialist in placentas, to measure the blood flow through the placenta, which was positive.

By Christmas, we had reached 22 weeks and so far, I had managed to keep the news from family and friends as I had been too scared to tell anybody or even get excited. I felt as if I was protecting myself and our baby by keeping the news a secret and lying low.

Less fuss, less talk, fewer worries, and more focus.

But by Christmas, I was ready to tell Ellie, Joel and my parents.

We had planned a family Christmas at my parents' house, but the government stopped households mixing, so in the end we told our news over Zoom!

I had little cards printed – the envelope said, 'Somebody wants to say hello' and then inside, there was a picture of our baby scan.

On the back, was written, 'Baby Preston-Adams, due 2nd May.'

A couple of days later, I noticed a lump or hardening just below my belly button. The consultant told us to return to the hospital. It was a small hernia but it turned out to be of no harm to me or the baby so once again it was a relief.

It also explained what the pain was when I was heavily pregnant with Bobby and it confirmed the midwife's earlier diagnosis had been right.

One mystery solved.

We continued lying low during lockdown and were only allowed to leave the house to work or for exercise, so it was a perfect time to be pregnant.

During my pregnancy with Bobby, Trevor and I both had hectic lives. Neither of us sat still for long. Lockdown forced us to relax and enjoy just being at home with each other and our dogs. Trevor was still able to go out to work every day but wasn't travelling far and was home every night.

I accepted the fact that I wasn't able to see Ellie and Joel due because of the restrictions; they were both working full time. I spoke to them a lot on FaceTime to keep up with their busy lives. They were both progressing amazingly; Ellie had a full-time marketing role and Joel was taking a degree apprenticeship in Project Management with onsite experience components.

Living near West Wittering meant we were lucky to be able to go for beautiful beach walks, or alternatively head in the other direction to the South Downs.
We both felt so lucky and would often have to remind ourselves, 'We live here!'

Trevor had been working on his guitar skills throughout lockdown and I'd been writing, so we kept ourselves occupied but life was calmer and I'm sure it helped the pregnancy.

The supportive hospital care continued.
We were scanned fortnightly, so we have an incredible bank of scan pictures from the moment of implantation, right through to the due date.
It was so incredible to be able to see our baby forming inside my womb, month by month.

Everything went smoothly and I was gradually telling more friends and relatives as my confidence grew. They were all delighted of course, and there was not long to wait as we were already way past halfway.

I also started to relax a bit more during scans as the continuous care helped with easing the trauma... until one of our visits revealed another new hurdle.

I was on the hospital scan bed for a routine scan when the sonographer said,

"You have a low-lying placenta, and the baby is lying traverse." It wasn't news the baby was traverse - that had been the case all the way through. But what was a low-lying placenta?

We were asked to sit in a waiting room and a short while later a nurse came to talk to us. She explained the dangers and risks of a low-lying placenta; not to be confused with placenta Previa, which sounded really dangerous, but still, it didn't sound good.

She handed us a leaflet, but all I remember reading were the words,

'There is a risk of haemorrhaging and may require a blood transfusion during C-section'. My heart started beating and I could feel myself going into a panic.

She explained: "This could happen later in the pregnancy, so you'd need to tell us immediately if you see any kind of bleeding. I'd advise you not to have sex to be on the safe side. Most low-lying placentas move upwards as the baby grows, so hopefully that will happen but we'll keep an eye on things."

I felt relieved that it wasn't placenta Previa as that really sounded frightening. I remained shaky when we left the hospital and felt tears swelling as we were leaving the building but they were soon washed away in one of Trevor's big bear hugs.

At the next few scans, we were hoping that the placenta had moved up but no, each time we were told, "The placenta is still lying low".

At our next visit from Fran, our midwife, we talked about our concerns. She explained that the risk of having a low-lying placenta was more towards the end of a pregnancy, after around 36 weeks.
But although not yet confirmed, we knew the C-section would be early, around 34 weeks, so the risk was removed. This helped us relax.

Time started flying by and the next time we saw Jan, before we even had time to sit down, he announced, "I have a C-section date for you! 34 (weeks) plus 2 (days)!" Trevor asked,
"What does that mean?" "Thirty-four weeks gestation plus two days."
"What date will that be?" I asked.

"That will be 23rd March and I will be doing your delivery." What a relief!

We had the most incredible sonographer at the appointment who managed to get angles which gave us a clear view of the baby's face. It was overwhelming and gave me hope.

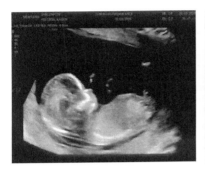 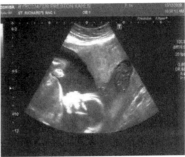

Chapter Twenty - Three: The Big Bleed

In the 10 days before the planned C-section, I distracted myself with house bits – I'd bought a couple of new rugs and with not long to go, I wanted to get all the niggly jobs done before we went to hospital.

I don't think I overdid it but I managed to get myself past the fear and excitement about our baby arriving soon.

At 5pm I was shattered so I went to bed for a snooze. I'd been asleep for about an hour and when I woke up, I sat upright.

As I moved, I felt a gush, like a heavy period. *Crikey*, I thought, *I hope this is a discharge (which I'd been having).*

Unfortunately, not, it was blood. I called Trevor, who was on a Zoom call with his whole family. "TREVOR!" I screamed. He came rushing out of the kitchen.

"I'm bleeding! It's heavy – we need to go to the hospital right now!"

He flew up the stairs and we both looked in the bathroom – it was even worse than I'd thought – there was blood on the floor and a big lump in the pan. Was it placenta?

"Babe, I know it's gross but would you mind grabbing it so we can take it with us to the doctor to find out what it is?" Without hesitation, he reached it and said, 'it's like a lump of flesh."

"OK let's put it in a food bag and bring it with us."

We drove while on the phone to the labour ward who asked whether we had called an ambulance.

"No, we're driving." Trevor replied.

"Has she got a towel?" Nope, I'd stuffed a handful of tissues in my underwear. I hadn't even looked at my jeans, but they felt wet with blood.

As we got into the car, I said,

"Please just put your foot down – don't worry about police." All sorts were going around my mind at this moment, but mostly, that I wasn't feeling any movement – I took deep breaths, trying to stay calm.

We were to head straight for A&E as the labour ward had instructed, and they'd meet us there.

"I can't feel any movement," I said to the nurse on the phone as I fought tears.

"Try not to worry," they said, but it felt impossible as this exactly the conversation I'd had two years ago when we'd lost Bobby. I hung up and tried to breathe.

A couple of minutes later my mobile went again; it was the hospital. "Are you going to Chichester or Worthing?" "Chichester."

"OK, don't go to A&E – just head straight for the labour ward – the team are waiting for you."

What felt like an eternity later (but was actually about 10 minutes) we pulled up outside the hospital. We couldn't get out of the car and into the building fast enough. The cold blood around my jeans chilled me through.

We got the lift to the labour ward door, where a nurse was waiting and as we entered, more nurses and a doctor appeared.
'I can't feel movement!'
It was like being in a horror movie. I was bent over, somehow thinking this would slow down the bleeding and keep hold of the baby.

The team helped us into a room – and my heart plummeted as I recognised where I was - the same room we'd spent our last hours with Bobby.

I looked at the doctor and said, "I had a stillborn baby two years ago."
"I know sweetheart," she replied gently. "Let's get you lying on the bed."

I pulled off my coat and threw it on the floor, scrambling onto the bed. I was so frightened and I had a flashback to when we were waiting to hear Bobby's heart.

I went into shock and felt as if I was going to pass out, then somebody was undressing me and somebody else was putting a cannula into my hand in preparation for a blood transfusion.

I needed to hear the heartbeat but all I could do was lie there and try not to pass out.

I felt dizzy and everything started to slow down as the nurse pushed the scan against my belly but finally there it was! The heartbeat!

"We're OK!" she said.

"A perfect heartbeat!"

I felt Trevor's lips on mine – he was sobbing. "Our baby is OK!" he said.

The doctor went through my notes and asked a list of questions about the reasons why I had seen various consultants (such as the placenta specialist) and about my children and number of pregnancies. I told them our story and the more I talked, the calmer I became.

The baby's heart rate meanwhile seemed to be getting a little faster.

'Have you eaten recently?" the doctor asked.

 "Not really," I said. "Trevor was in the middle of making a shepherd's pie when the bleed came so we hadn't got to dinner yet."

"Ok, let's get some food into you and I think the heart rate will then decrease."

And she was absolutely right. I had a very tasty egg sandwich and the baby's heart rate steadied.

It was decided that the safest course of action for me was to stay in for observation as it seemed the placenta had now dropped even lower and had become the dreaded Placenta Previa. Bleeding with this condition was common and could easily happen again.

Trevor went home to collect some overnight things for me and I was taken downstairs to the maternity ward.

The overnight stay felt strange. I was checked on every few hours along with the baby's heartbeat. It was only a week until our scheduled C-section so not long to go.

The next day I took things easy; my meals were brought to me and I knew not to rush around. I started gradually to get my bits ready for going home and lay in bed waiting while working on my laptop.

The bleeding had darkened and dried, so all was looking good until around 6pm when I popped to the toilet and there was a small amount of fresh blood.

I mentioned it to one of the midwives and a few minutes later, a doctor appeared and suggested I stay again overnight just to be safe.

I agreed and messaged Trevor.

One more night turned into 10 days. A doctor said, "You've come so far, what would happen if you had another haemorrhage and the ambulance took time, or you were stuck in traffic getting here? We don't know how the baby would cope with another bleed so I would recommend you stay in. Your C-section is booked for next Tuesday anyway and there would be no time wasted whizzing you up for an emergency C-section if we needed to."

As he was talking, I knew he was right. I missed Trevor and the dogs but this was absolutely the correct thing to do.

At least I could still work to keep myself busy; I'd have to tell my boss and finish work on Friday but I could still try to achieve a good handover. I knew I didn't need to but I wanted to.

I asked a midwife if there was anywhere to hold Zoom meetings for work and an hour or so later, nurses came back and said they were moving me to my own room. I felt super-lucky with my own sofa, a wardrobe and private bathroom, my new home for just over a week.

The days rolled into one.

Trevor and the dogs would come and collect me every day to go for a walk, so I got fresh air and exercise, but my anxiety got worse and worse.

I was petrified about the C-section and tried to keep distracted because every time I thought about it, I cried.

I moved back into the main ward as the private room was needed and I kept my spirits up, trying not to let my feelings show because I didn't want to create a 'thing' about it.

I saved my tears for Trevor instead and let them out on our walks.

The day before the C-section was scheduled, I felt my tummy tightening. When I walked back in through the door to the maternity ward, I burst into tears and the midwife checked the baby heartbeat.

What a relief, it was still strong!

Not even 24 hours to go; I just needed to hang in there a little bit longer.

Chapter Twenty - Four: The Big Day!

Surprisingly I'd managed to get some sleep overnight despite the nerves.

"I should be feeling excited," I thought. "Today's the day we'll finally meet our baby after such a journey." But I couldn't feel any excitement through the fear of surgery. With Placenta Previa, the op was in the worst-case scenario, life threatening due to the risk of heavy bleeding, plus there could be the need for a full hysterectomy, which I didn't want.

I was put on the heart monitor first thing in the morning and then had an hour to get showered, dressed, and pack my belongings. I was rushing around so much, the nerves started to subside.

Jan, our consultant, popped by to say hello and talk through the next steps – we were first on the list for the elective (planned) C-sections so as long as there were no emergencies, we'd be first.

Kirsty, one of the midwives, explained that she was going to be with us in the theatre. I'd been thinking over the past week that I'd recognised her and wondered if she looked after our C-section with Bobby but didn't ask her as I didn't want to go there.

Trevor arrived at 8:30am, as I was heading up to the labour ward. I'd collected quite a few bags over the past week so had lots to carry. Trevor had brought his new camera so he had a few bags too!

We were shown into a little room where we'd do initial checks and get settled. A few doctors came and introduced themselves, and we were told that we could create a playlist of music for when we would be in the operating theatre. So that became Trevor's job. We both love a country music, so we had some Kenny Rogers and as Trevor is a Bruce Springsteen fan, a bit of Bruce was added as well.

Kirsty left the room for a few moments and when she returned, she said, "I didn't realise until I saw Trevor, but I looked after you when you had Bobby."
"I was wondering that," I replied, and touched her arm.
"If you'd prefer me to get another midwife to go to the theatre with you, I'd completely understand."
"Not at all," I replied. "It's lovely that you can come in with us, as long as you're happy to be with us again."

We waited for a couple of hours because of emergency cases coming in, which was perfect as it gave Trevor and I time together before the operation. By the time Jan popped in to do a quick scan I was tranquil.

He wanted to know which position the baby was in. Until now, the baby had always been lying transverse (horizontally) in all the scans but this morning was lying head down – maybe he or she was ready for us!

Then came our moment and we went through to the theatre – my tummy was in knots and I was petrified all over again. I was given the epidural and was expecting either to die or need a hysterectomy.

"Well, here we go!"

I clutched Trevor's hand as the procedure began and could feel lots of tugging and pulling around… then Jan announced. "OK, I have a baby. I'll hold him up so you can see whether we have a boy or a girl." And there he was! Our miracle rainbow baby, Archie Preston Adams, born on 23rd March 2021, weighing 5lb 1oz. We both burst into tears; what an incredible moment after such a harrowing journey. In that instant, all the pain was worth it, every injection, and every setback.

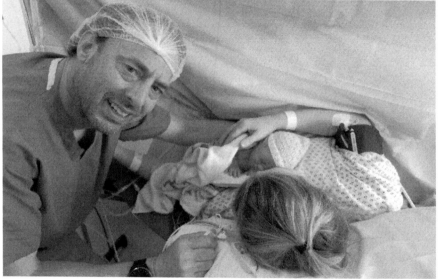

As Trevor and I hugged our new precious baby, Trevor said, "He looks like Bobby." And he did! I've since compared the lock of Bobby's hair we kept with Archie's.

The room was ecstatic and everybody was emotional; I'm pretty sure I saw tears in Jan's eyes too. It was almost impossible to take in – our very own take-home baby.

Trevor cut the cord but for me the fear now really kicked in. I knew this was a dangerous time as the placenta also had to be born and this was when I could have heavy bleeding.

I felt more tugging and pulling and pushing and I took deep breaths for what felt like ages. Meanwhile, Trevor was off taking photos (surprise, surprise!) and finally came back to hold my hand again.

There was a doctor sitting behind me who had been controlling the drugs and fluids going into my body. I couldn't see what was going on down below so throughout the procedure, he was giving me a running commentary about what was happening.

"How are things going with the placenta?" I asked, after what felt like an eternity,

"It's out," replied the doctor. "It's out?" I repeated in disbelief.

"Yes, the stitches are being done now – you're nearly all done!"

"I'M ALIVE! AND STILL WITH ALL MY BODY PARTS!" I almost couldn't believe it. I cried again. We had done it! Our consultant Jan was a genius.

Archie and I stayed in hospital for another two weeks and were well cared for until he was strong enough to come home. Going home with our very own baby was the most magical moment of our lives. We cried for most of the first week.

Of course, there were and still are times when we think of Bobby. It is heart-breaking to think that we didn't get to take him home too.
We will never fully recover from his loss and I still wonder, or perhaps want to believe, that Bobby's spirit is in Archie's body.

When I drive past the crematorium or the funeral parlour, my heart aches as I remember having to sign those papers and then say goodbye to our sleeping baby.
Many times, I have cried when reading stories to Archie because I so desperately wanted to read them to Bobby.
Sometimes I can't finish songs I'm singing to Archie because I wanted to sing them to our baby Bobby too.

Even as I'm writing this section of the book, tears stream as I explain how I'm affected. But this is it, the reality of losing a baby and I'm OK with the truth that sometimes I still need to cry.
I'll always hurt and miss him.

But finally, we have our Rainbow Baby, our precious miracle rainbow baby, Archie Preston Adams.

PART SIX

Chapter Twenty - Five – In a Nutshell

If telling our story helps just one person, then it was a story worth telling.

Although we did get the happy ending that we wanted and planned, I am very aware that not everybody does.

Some people go on to adopt children and some people decide that actually having children just isn't meant to be. And that's also great!

These are success stories, just of a different kind.

Here are a few points that I'd like to highlight, which I've learned or that helped me on our journey.

General things I have learned:

The Coil: When you have the coil fitted, the doctor may ask you if you'd like the string snipped. I'd advise you to say no because that's what caused our issues getting the coil removed; there wasn't enough string for easy removal.

Egg freezing: If time is ticking and you think you may want children in the future, look into having your eggs frozen – this will help eliminate the time panic if you end up wanting to have children in your late 30s or 40s (or older these days).

Older mums: Never judge people for being an older mum! You don't know how long that woman has been trying for her child or her children.

Distractions: If you are on a fertility journey, try to plan things which are non-related, to try to distract. It's impossible not to worry, or to be anxious, but if you can try to keep things going in the background it can help to relieve the pressure; whether it's work, or booking holidays / breaks – going out to the cinema, massages etc.

Keeping secrets: Everybody has different ways of dealing with situations, but in the end, I found it much easier not to tell anybody at all when we were having IVF and kept our pregnancies a secret for as long as I could.

Things I did differently for the last successful round of IVF:

Having IVF is not for the faint hearted! There are lots of injections, drugs and sacrifices involved. Although it wasn't easy, the experience was fascinating. Trevor and I both learned so much about reproduction and the incredible things that can be done to help people have children.

In the end, I actually felt safer having IVF than having a natural pregnancy because the eggs, the embryos and then the pregnancies are monitored so closely, right from the day the eggs and sperm are produced. Some of the things I did differently for our final IVF round were:

- Exercise – I was determined to be super fit and strong ready for the last try at IVF. I did yoga, running, cycling, and swimming as much as I could every day.
- I stopped caffeine altogether the month before.
- I stopped alcohol the month before.
- We used embryo glue.
- We used steroids to prevent my body rejecting the pregnancy.
- I took it really, really easy for the 72 hours following embryo transfer, to allow the embryo to stick to the womb.

Things that I did differently during my successful pregnancy with Archie:

Our bodies are all different and no two pregnancies are the same but I noted some of the things that I did during our successful pregnancy with Archie, just in case you might like to give any of them a go. You never know!

- Vitamins: I drank a Complan build-up milkshake every morning from embryo transfer day for a good supply of vitamins and calcium. I used semi-skimmed milk until the third trimester.
- I drank LOTS of water.
- I prayed! I found a few prayers for pregnant women and read them every few days.
- I completely stopped exercising.
- I avoided stressful situations.
- I hardly left the house.

Also, rest, rest, rest. Up until embryo transfer I was dedicated to getting my body fit. I jogged 2-4 miles per day, cycling, swimming and doing yoga; pretty much every day. I needed my body to be strong.

On the day of embryo transfer I was advised to stop all exercise, even yoga.

Rest, rest, rest, Hakan advised.

During my final pregnancy, Covid had hit, and I (the entire country) was forced to stay at home and not meet other households to prevent the spread of the disease. That suited me fine for the safety of my pregnancy.

I'm quite sure that's how my body coped so well with Archie's pregnancy.

So again, I'd advise to rest, rest, and rest.

Chapter Twenty - Six – Advice for Friends and Family

Throughout our journey, I realised that our miscarriages and the loss of our baby Bobby didn't just affect us, it massively affected our close friends and family. How can they help after such tragedies or what can they say to make things easier? Ellie once said: "What can I say when there are no words?" And how right she was.

Things that helped:

The care, kindness and inclusivity of our family and friends was second to none. Our families were always in touch, dropping kind messages, and friends travelled down to see us, just to 'be'. We were open and talked to people, trying not to overload them because it was a lot to share. But we never felt under any pressure for anything.

I really appreciated people inviting us to events: to dinner, evening drinks and not giving up on us when we kept declining. It just took us time to get ourselves back up on our feet.

Having maternity leave as normal helped massively. It took the stress off returning to work. Then, when I did return, I was hugely supported by colleagues. It took a little while to build up my confidence to face the world and my colleagues helped me move forwards into my new normal.

Things which didn't help:

"Your worrying and being obsessive is probably blocking your ability to conceive." This is something I really didn't appreciate, and I touched on this in our story. Not only did this hurt inside, it infuriated me!

Worry and anxiety aren't like light switches that can be turned off. I would advise everybody to avoid saying this to anybody desperate to become pregnant. Instead, be supportive.

Negativity:

People saying, "Maybe it just isn't meant to be" when they see how hard you're trying to become a mum, this is also very hurtful. Positivity is a powerful thing – it's important that people around you share positivity when you're going through a journey like this.

Useful Resources:

Sands UK – www.sands.org.uk

Tommy's – www.tommys.org

Ask Me His Name by Elle Wright – An amazing book

Eat yourself pregnant by Zita West – Available on Amazon

Gateway women –www.gateway-women.com for childless women.

APPENDIX

How can we ever thank those who helped us on our journey? Here is the email I sent to consultants Jan Inder Rieden and Melanie Tipples just after Archie was born.

Dear Jan and Mel,

Well, What a journey! How can we ever thank you enough?

You have both been hugely instrumental in helping us finally get our dream rainbow baby and it will always be remembered. Jan, I actually think you performed some kind of miracle in that theatre; I was so ready for a much worse scenario - and you made it all seem so easy!

Archie is doing so well; he's in a big boy cot now and has started breastfeeding. I'm mending really well too - with only a tiny amount of bleeding!

I attach some photos of theatre Mel. It will give you an idea of the amazing atmosphere in theatre that day - it was surreal yet so amazing.

There are no words to express how thankful we are.
Lots of love, Karen, Trevor, and Archie xx

After such a heart-wrenching and exhausting journey, I'm proud of us. We pushed and pushed until we got what we wanted. And now... life, well it's pretty perfect.

We are living our dream as a newly married couple with our beautiful rainbow baby and our two dogs by the seaside.

Thank you to our support network. We are surrounded by amazing people. In no particular order:

Medical and Alternative Health Professionals:

Dr Jan Inder Rieden: Our consultant at St Richard's Hospital:

Jan has travelled most of this journey with us. Jan was sadly the last person to hear Bobby's heartbeat and had the heart-wrenching job of telling us. From our first meeting, Jan's support has been incredible. From checking out IVF clinics abroad to booking us in for scans, we certainly put this man through his paces but it was incredibly comforting knowing that we were in good hands and the level of support was second to none.

Ms Melanie Tipples - Our Consultant, Nuffield Hospital:

Initially, we met Ms Tipples when I was diagnosed with an ovarian cyst, at the beginning of our IVF journey. From there she was on standby, giving us support and reassurance.

Inga Maynard - Midwife who helped us through Baby Bobby's delivery:

I have no idea how nurses like Inga have enough strength for their jobs. I certainly couldn't do it. She helped us through the worst time of our lives and I couldn't have been without her.

I can't put the trauma of that day into words but she was one of the few people who got to see and hold baby Bobby. I will never forget Inga, her strength and support, as long as I live.

She's an amazing human being.

Gill Bescoby - Acupuncture Specialist:

I was introduced to Gill a few weeks after we had lost Bobby. Gill became another support for Trevor and I.

I saw her twice a week sometimes but usually weekly and she was the one person I was honest with about my feelings.

Some days I'd sit down with her and burst into tears, just because, and that was OK. She helped me work things out, kept me calm and on an even keel (a challenge in itself!)

Sally - Masseuse:

Sally is a fantastic masseuse - she still comes to us and she gives incredible massages and helpful advice. I firmly believe that massages help with fertility and general health. During our IVF journey, Sally came up with some suggestions; one was to drink lots of water, which sounds self-explanatory, but for somebody to point it out made me more conscious of the amounts of water I was drinking.

Also, Sally suggested saying little prayers. As a Catholic, I thought I'd give this a go and I found some short fertility prayers and said them every day throughout the last cycle of IVF and... well, we have Archie now!

Nicole - Team Miracle IVF Coordinator:

I can't compliment or give enough credit to Nicole. Imagine dealing with many women and couples desperately trying to have a baby with time running out, hormonal, frightened, frustrated, anxious, tired, desperate and goodness knows what else.

She keeps them calm, answering all their emotional, medical and travel questions - even tackling the whole Covid-19 travel restriction questions and frustrations. It must be such a tough job. Nicole was on standby from the first point of contact.

At one point through the lockdown, I was sending her questions first thing in the morning, thinking she was in Cyprus (two hours ahead) but she wasn't. She was in the UK answering them at 7am! She has her own family to co-ordinate and still managed to support me.

Her answers were always prompt, clear, and made sense. If she didn't know the answer, she'd find out as soon as physically possible. She really is an incredible lady. Nicole, thank you. So very much. You are my IVF rock.

Friends:

It's difficult being a friend to somebody who has suffered the trauma of losing a baby. What do you do? How do you help? Well, you can't really; you can just be an ear to listen, a shoulder to cry on and a presence of being there for wobbles which will happen, some days and weeks more than others.

I am blessed to be surrounded by friends who, without exception, have been supportive and loving throughout this journey. Where would I be without you?

Tiff Mulcahy. Absolute Solid Bestie:

We all have a crazy friend who's non-judgemental and solid and that's Tiff in a nutshell. During our darkest days, I'd sometimes message her in the middle of the night, having a meltdown and within minutes she'd calm me. Tiff has always been and always will be my go-to.

Tiff's journey has by no means been easy so far either. I just hope that through life, I have also been enough of a friend to her in return.

My Parents:

Being an only child, I am my parents' world. Any pain I feel, they feel, and they have been there through thick and thin. I'd like to think that my children feel that safety net too.

There have been times where I've wondered how much more I can put my parents through, and so try to prevent further worry. But they always know if there are things going on. I'd like to publicly thank my parents for being the special, caring, and loving people they are. I'd like to thank my dad for giving me my patient side and thank my mum for my strength because, without doubt, it is my mum who gave it to me.

Our Extended Family:

For those of you who are lucky enough to be part of a large family, you'll understand how special it is. Not just at weddings, christenings, communions, even funerals, but all of the time. I'm super lucky to have many cousins, aunts, and uncles who I love very much and who, again, have always been there. I'd like them all to know how much I appreciate them.

Work, Colleagues, and Work Friends.

My colleagues from *Towards Maturity* joined my journey with Bobby and each person from that company offered support. When I returned to work after the maternity break, they treated me with care and respect, and made my return possible.

Clarissa Hall: My colleague was the first person I called after finding out we'd lost Bobby. We were due at a meeting if I remember rightly. It was a call we are both unlikely ever to forget. Clarissa is such an amazing person to work with.

Jonathan Burden: Who became my boss and mentor when I returned and managed me so well. I looked forward to getting up in the mornings and getting to my job. That was down to his excellent management skills which will never be forgotten. He gave me focus and support.

Support from our parent company itself, *Emerald Publishing*, at the time of losing Bobby, and then through several cycles of IVF was unbelievable. The CEO of our business at the time, Peter Casebow, was incredible, extremely supportive and understanding.

Lauren Taylor: Dog Walker and Housekeeper.

Last on the list but by no means last in priority. Lauren has been such a pleasure to know generally. I confided a lot in Lauren because I saw her twice a week. Bella and Bonita go mad when she arrives. She has been a tower of support and the dogs love her. In addition, she has become a good friend.

Glossary:

IUI - Intrauterine insemination (IUI) is a fertility treatment that involves directly inserting sperm into a woman's womb. So basically, it's not IVF but it's saving the sperm from having to travel to the womb itself.

ICSI – (Intracytoplasmic Sperm Injection). This is what we had on every IVF cycle. It is an IVF technique in which a single sperm is injected into the centre of an egg.

hCG LEVELS - Human chorionic gonadotropin (hCG) is a hormone produced by the body during pregnancy. It supports fetal growth. Doctors test hCG levels in the urine and blood to confirm pregnancy. They also use hCG blood tests to help determine if a person could be experiencing an ectopic pregnancy or miscarriage.

AMH LEVELS – (Anti-Müllerian Hormone). An AMH test is a useful indicator of eggs remaining in a woman's ovarian reserve. A 'normal' AMH level is considered to be 1.0 ng/mL to 3.0 ng/mL. Low AMH is considered to be an AMH below 0.9 ng/ml.

Biography

I never thought I would write a book about fertility, or even write a book at all! But life has a funny way of navigating us where it wants us to go, despite our best-laid plans. So, I have become a writer, to help break the taboos around child loss, stillbirth, and fertility issues. I've written Feathers & Rainbows as it was the book I needed when I was going through my journey of hope and loss.

I'm just an ordinary girl - well, woman. I married young and had two children in my twenties and thought that was that until I divorced. At that time, I missed having little children around so much that I considered solo adoption... and then I met Trevor, the love of my life. The new relationship confirmed that I did indeed want more children with this beautiful man, and we wanted our own if that was possible. But I knew the odds were stacked against us - I was in my late thirties by this stage, and Trevor was in his late forties.

All we could do was try and hope for the best. That hope set us on a several years-long journey that included every obstacle and adversity imaginable: medical challenges, age issues, incompetent IVF in the UK, international IVF, COVID19, numerous miscarriages, and the tragic stillbirth of our full-term baby, Bobby.

I was compelled to write Feathers & Rainbows to share our journey in vivid detail as there are still so many taboos when speaking about baby loss and fertility as an "older couple". It's often still expected that couples, particularly women, grieve in silence and move on quickly. Unfortunately, the out-of-sight-out-of-mind and stiff-upper-lip approaches fail to recognise the profound loss experienced, including the loss of future hopes and dreams. It is prevalent and toxic in our society, but the narrative is slowly shifting as women and couples speak more openly about their experiences.

We were lucky and so grateful to have our happy ending with the birth of our rainbow baby, Archie. His smiling face has made the journey worth it for us, but there are still fragments of our hearts that will never heal.

Our wish for Feathers & Rainbows is that it will comfort those on a fertility journey, those grieving a loss, or even those forced to find a different "happy ending". I sincerely hope that you will find comfort in reading my story and know you are not alone in the midst of the most stressful and, at times, heart-breaking life experiences.

I also want to acknowledge that there are many happy endings possible even if there is no baby to show for it at the end. There needs to be more space for child-free narratives in our society. Everyone deserves to know there is gold waiting at the end of the rainbow, with or without a baby.

Printed in Poland
by Amazon Fulfillment
Poland Sp. z o.o., Wrocław
17 December 2021

bdfd78c4-e770-4bea-8db0-6e04473da014R01